Puppy T

MW00928466

Puppy Training For Beginners

A Simple User's Guide To Housebreaking, Obedience Training And Crate Training Your Puppy In Days

Table of Contents

Introduction

In this book you will find lots of useful tips on how to become an effective trainer so your puppy can grow up to be a well-rounded pup in the future.

We've included everything you'll ever need to know about crate training, potty training and housebreaking. We've even included a few basic commands that your pup will easily understand and obey.

Now all you need is to go through each chapter and understand it as best as you can and then try it out on your pup. Within a couple of days you should be able to see some improvement!

Let's begin the journey.

Chapter 1: Becoming A Good Puppy Trainer

Bringing home a puppy is the start of a lifelong relationship. Your puppy is going to depend on you for everything and in turn he will give you all the love you will ever need.

What's your motivation?

To become a good puppy trainer, you will have to examine yourself and find out what your motivation is for training your puppy. Are you planning on having him joindog shows where you can both show off your advanced tricks? Perhaps you're looking to enter your puppy into the military or police service so he can serve his nation? Or do you just want to have a well behaved puppy who will obey your every command?

Whatever your motivation is, you will have to ensure that strict discipline is followed at all times and positive reinforcement is used all throughout the training to retain good behaviors and weed out the bad ones.

Becoming the Alpha

Taking our cue from the world's leading dog psychology experts, you will have to establish yourself as the alpha in your pack. As the alpha, you are the one your puppy is going to look towards for instructions or to affirm his emotional state.

What you will need to develop is a calm and assertive personality that dogs easily identify with.

You have to understand that dogs, no matter how intelligent they may seem, don't really understand the English language (or any human language for that matter). What they understand though is your gestures and distinct sounds you make when giving a command.

So, you will have to ensure that your commands sound very different from each other if you expect your dog to follow spoken word commands.

We'll go into that more as we progress through this book.

Your puppy is going to test your resolve each step of the way and you have to make sure that you practice discipline at all times. You will have to resist his charms when he makes a mistake if you expect him to understand that what he is doing isn't the behavior you expect at the time that he commits a mistake.

Taking care of your puppy

First things first, your puppy isn't a toy that you just call to entertain you or to command. He is a living being who has his unique personality and basic wants and needs. He also has his own unique attitude. No two puppies are quite alike.

It is in your best interest to keep your puppy happy, healthy and strong so that you won't have any issues during training sessions. A happy puppy is motivated to learn as well as keep you happy. This is a good combination for a teachable puppy.

Food

To ensure that your puppy grows up into a healthy adult, you will have to make sure that you feed him the right amount of food from the start. At 3 months old, he will already be weaned off from his mother which is just the right time to introduce solid or semi-solid food into his diet.

Try to provide raw meat every once in a while to add protein to his diet. Include some bones for him to chew on which should help maintain strong and healthy teeth.

Shelter

For shelter, a puppy only needs a space big enough for him to turn around in, stand up or sit without feeling cramped. A good start is with a crate (and we will discuss this at length under the crate training chapter).

Make sure that your puppy's shelter or home is sturdy enough to withstand his rambunctiousness and warm enough for him to get comfortable in at night. It doesn't have to be fancy. Four walls and a sturdy floor with a soft, warm blanket for a bed should suffice.

Make sure you clean his shelter out every 2 or 3 days and spray it with anti-mite and lice solution to reduce the risk of these bugs bothering your puppy. You can also wash his blanket and place it under the sun to get rid of any lice and mite eggs as well as lessen the puppy dour that's going to develop from constant use.

Grooming

Grooming is essential for your puppy's health and well-being. It is in your best interest to have a clean, healthy and happy puppy so that you won't have any issues during training.

Maintaining your puppy's fur - Your puppy needs constant grooming (especially if they're the long haired variety) to maintain his overall health and happiness. Depending on his age, give your puppy a regular bath once or twice a month to keep his fur clean. Make sure you blow dry and wipe him off with a towel to remove excess moisture. A quick brushing session once or twice a week should remove tangles and matted fur.

Maintaining your puppy's teeth – You will also have to check his teeth to keep them clean and away from any possible dental issues that could impact his health.

Maintaining your puppy's claws – your puppy has claws that will grow over time and this can impede his mobility if they grow too long. Make it a point to teach your puppy that clipping his claws is not something to be afraid of.

Exercise

It's a known fact that dogs love to walk. They simply can't live without it. And giving your dog some exercise is an essential part of your relationship with your puppy.

Simply letting your puppy off his leash in your backyard isn't going to be enough. He needs a structured exercise more than just a carefree romp in the garden.

Through walks, you can establish your role as the alpha while your puppy faithfully follows at your side or behind you. 30 minutes' walk (minimum) should be enough to wean off the excess energy your puppy builds up over time.

Try to match your exercise with the type of breed your dog belongs. Some dogs need more physical activity than others and you don't want to unnecessarily exhaust your puppy.

Basic Tools of the trade

Collar

One of the most important things that you need to invest in for your puppy is a good collar. Get your puppy used to wearing a collar as soon as you get him so that you won't have any issues while training him. You can use the collar to attach his leash to or to control him if he becomes too rambunctious.

The collar can also be a point of attachment for a dog tag which should include your name, address and a number people can contact you with. This is extremely important because there have been a lot of cases when a puppy simply just runs away during training sessions and gets lost.

Leash

A good leash is also important for training your puppy. Get a sturdy leash that can handle your puppy's weight. Adjust the type of leash you use as he grows older.

Clicker

Most dog trainers use a clicker for positive reinforcement and it has shown good results in training your puppy. This is a great tool to reinforce positive behaviors but is not necessary as you can replicate the sound of a clicker through snapping your finger.

You can buy a clicker at most pet shops or you can simply create one by using the cover of a mayonnaise jar.

Whistle

A whistle is another device that has been used by trainers for a very long time and it has also shown great results. This is also an optional device if you know how to whistle with your lips. There is a far greater range of sounds you can produce just by whistling with your lips instead of using this tool. The only advantage a whistle has on you is that it can produce a far louder sound if you blow hard enough. Whistling with your lips doesn't also come naturally for most people.

You can buy a whistle from virtually any store. Make sure it is able to produce a loud sound that can travel over long distances.

Treats

A vast majority of dogs respond well to treats especially while training. Using treats as a reward can help you keep your puppy's attention on you at all times during training sessions. Giving your puppy treats for good behaviors will also help him realize that what he's doing is good and constant repetition of the behavior means getting a treat.

Have a big bag of treats ready at all times. You can buy treats from any pet store, grocer or mall in your area. You can also create homemade treats which should be far more nutritionally sound than mass produced treats on the shelves of the aforementioned stores.

Spray bottle

One very useful tool in correcting bad behavior is using a spray bottle with water in it. Simply direct a jet of water towards your puppy if he misbehaves. The water won't harm him and it will immediately get his attention.

An empty bottle with marbles or pebbles in it

An empty bottle with pebbles or marbles in it is another example of an unconventional training tool that you don't see often. The contents of the bottle will rattle inside and create a noise that can get your dog's attention immediately if he misbehaves.

Do not use this tool for puppies or dogs who are high strung as it can lead to panic attacks and could be detrimental to his training. You can use this when he is older and is used to strange sights and sounds around him.

Basic training techniques and tools to train your puppy

There are many training techniques and tools that trainers all over the world use to successfully teach puppies and dogs alike how to respond appropriately to spoken word commands.

Assume a calm assertive energy when handling your puppy

The most important thing that you as a trainer should develop is a calm and assertive energy. Dogs and puppies alike respond well to people who are calm and assertive because this is how dogs teach each other in the wild.

Before interacting with your puppy, make sure you leave all your stressful energy behind. Close your eyes, and then sit or stand in a comfortable position, and breathe in and out deeply at least ten times before handling your puppy. This shouldn't take long and you'll immediately feel a change in your outward energy.

Never handle a dog or puppy if you are stressed out and always keep your emotions in check when you're training them. Any change in your over-all emotional state will quickly be reflected back to you by your dog because they are very sensitive to these energy fields.

You will also need to practice a lot of patience during every training session. If you feel that you are slipping, simply do the breathing exercise again and you should feel better immediately.

Using your voice and the importance of speaking clearly

Since you will be using spoken word commands, it is imperative that you speak clearly so that your puppy will understand what it is that you want from him.

Open your mouth and issue the command with an even volume and tone. Do not raise your voice if your puppy does not understand what you want him to do immediately. Instead, repeat the command with evenly spaced intervals.

Last but not the least: Never shout at your dog.

Use hand gestures and other physical cues

Hand gestures are just as important as spoken word commands. Hand gestures can complement your voice commands and make the puppy learn faster. Puppies also learn through visual methods. Using physical gestures will help your puppy create an association between the spoken word command and the gesture given.

Prepare lots of treats, praises and other rewards for good behaviour

Most dogs respond well to treats as a reward. You can buy a bag of doggie treats from your local grocer. You can also prepare home cooked treats which are far more nutritionally balanced and good for your puppy's health.

Additionally, you can reward your puppy simply by giving him a pat or a rub on the head. This type of reward can also be adjusted depending on your level of excitement and the amount of praise you want to heap on your puppy. For example: if he did a really good job, increase the vigor of the rubbing motion to express extreme pleasure. You can also pat other parts of their body to signify delight. Dogs love to be touched everywhere but there are special spots that they love the most like their head, chest and belly.

Scratching their necks and bellies is also a good form of reward.

Reserve patting their behinds for correcting posture.

Another form of reward that seems to work well with all dogs is a spoken word reward. A simple "good boy" or "good girl" will suffice. Try to use this reward with a higher than usual pitch and tone of voice.

Other rewards can come in the form of giving your puppy a toy to play with. You can also use this toy as a motivational tool to make training more effective.

Blocking

Another fairly new idea that has made training easier is the blocking technique. This is basically the act of physically blocking your pup.

This is done by standing directly in front of your puppy. Their natural reaction to this is to stop. Some puppies may sit to look up to you (this is a good technique to use when teaching your puppy how to "sit"). What this basically says to your puppy is that you are the dominant creature in the room and that he cannot move unless you want him to.

Blocking can be used in several ways. You can also use this to stop your puppy from pulling on his leash or from being aggressive towards other animals.

You can also use the environment for blocking exercises or use a stick to block his way (A walking stick is a good tool) if he tries to overtake you.

To end this chapter, here are some other things to consider tomake your life with your puppy a very happy one:

Be committed

Never get a puppy or a dog for a pet if you cannot fully commit to caring for it. Without commitment, you will not be able to train your pet effectively. You have to develop a deep level of commitment to bond with your puppy and efficiently train him to become the perfect dog in the future.

Before getting a puppy, ask yourself this question a hundred times: "are you ready to take on full responsibility for your puppy's health and well-being for his entire life?"

This is a very serious commitment because dogs leave at an average of about 10 to 12 years old. This is a long time for most people to stay particularly committed to something or someone.

If you said yes, then it's time to make an investment to honour the commitment. Make sure you have all the necessary tools and equipment to help you in caring for your puppy. Make sure you also develop your own personality to be able to handle your puppy's unique personality and the challenges you will face when training him. Last but not the least: make a commitment to love your puppy no matter what happens.

Never give up

Training requires time and a lot of patience. Your patience is going to get tested time and again during the training phase. It will also get tested once your puppy has grown up into an adult dog.

You have to remember that your dog does not come with a remote control and his level of understanding is going to be based entirely on how well you trained him while he was a puppy.

Spend a lot of time training your puppy to follow commands exactly as you want him to so that you won't have a grown up dog that doesn't know how to behave properly.

If your puppy does not understand what you want him to do immediately, don't give up. Keep on repeating the training sessions until he finally gets what you want him to do.

There's a difference between giving up and retiring the puppy for the next training session. Training sessions at the start can be anywhere from 5 to 15 minutes. You should know how to time the training exercises so that you can spot when your puppy is no longer motivated. At this point, stop the training exercise and try again later or tomorrow.

If your puppy is still motivated to work with you, then it means there's a breakdown in the communication. So, you either have to make your commands clearer or use gestures to make him understand better.

Do not give up on your puppy, he wants to please you. He just might be too tired to follow your command or does not understand what you're trying to tell him to do.

Be positive.

This can be applied to everything in your life. Having a positive attitude at all times will help you overcome frustrations and other stumbling blocks that might be in your way when you are trying to accomplish something.

Your pet is extremely sensitive to strong emotions. If you are frustrated or angry, he will feel it and may cower away from you. If you're anxious he will feel anxious as well.

But, if you have a positive energy, your puppy will feel it and he will be more eager to please you. Encouraging your pet to accomplish more is also easier if you have a positive attitude while doing the training exercises.

In conclusion, be committed, never give up and be positive!

Chapter 2: Crate Training

If you've done your research before getting a puppy, you've probably heard of crate training a lot by now. What is crate training and why is it so important?

Crate training is simply the act of using a crate (or any ample sized box enclosure) to temporarily house your puppy. This process helps make training easier and will also allow your puppy to build his confidence slowly but surely.

Effects of crate training

When your puppy is first separated from his mother and his littermates, he is going to feel very insecure and stressed out. Adding separation anxiety to the mix makes it even worse.

Placing a cloth inside the crate with his mother's and littermates' scent will help ease the transition between being with his family and becoming a part of yours.

Aside from that, a crate allows for easy transport from his original home to yours. It lessens the risk of your new puppy from making a mess inside your car because he got nervous.

Once you reach your home, the crate can act as a place for comfort for your puppy as he gets acquainted to your place. He may try to venture out every now and then and it will be a good thing for him to have a place he can retreat to if he feels uncomfortable in any way.

Crate training can make potty training and housebreaking an easier process as your puppy is wont to mess his immediate surroundings.

How to crate train your puppy

Crate training your puppy starts from the time you choose him from the litter until you bring him home. This process continues for a couple more weeks after that.

Crate training for puppies 3 months and below

When you go visit your puppy from your local breeder, bring an ample sized box or container which will serve as his crate. You can choose to leave the crate at the breeder's place or bring it along each time you visit.

If you've already chosen the puppy you want, try to ask the breeder to provide a temporary separation fence so you can spend time with the puppy without removing him entirely from his mother and littermates. Bring the crate inside this enclosure and try to get him acquainted with the scent. At this point, he may or may not enter the crate on his own volition. Don't rush this process. Allow him to familiarize himself with the scent of the crate. This can take anywhere between 3 days to a few weeks before he begins to trust the crate. This process should be started as soon as the puppy has begun to open his eyes. Try to keep these sessions short. A couple of minutes at a time should be enough for the puppy to get acquainted with the crate.

Crate training for puppies 3 months and up

At 3 months old, he should be ready to leave his family and become a part of yours. By now, your puppy is able to walk and run clumsily and has begun to become more curious about his surroundings.

Bring the crate inside the enclosure but this time stuff a piece of cloth with his mother's scent inside the crate. This should pique his curiosity and make him want to enter the crate. There will be a few tentative attempts before he finally enters the crate completely. When he does this on his own, give him a treat and praise him. Allow the puppy to come out and repeat the process again. This may take some time as these sessions should only be a couple of minutes long.

You can also speed up the process by simply using a treat to get him to go inside the crate. Place a treat near his nose and then lead him towards the crate. Place the treat inside the crate and allow him to enter on his own free will to get to the treat. Once he is inside, give him a treat and praise him for a job well done. Lead him out again by enticing him with a treat so you can repeat the process.

Once he is accustomed to the crate, it is time to close the door as soon as he is inside. Just repeat the process of getting him inside with a treat and then reward him with some praises. Wait for him to calm down and then slowly close the door while at the same time giving him some praises. After a few seconds open the door and let him out. Reward him with some treats and some praises for a job well done. Repeat the process over and over until he trusts the crate completely even with the door closed.

Never ever slam the door on the puppy while crate training is going on.

The basics to getting your puppy in and out of the crate:

The crate is going to be an unfamiliar object for your puppy and it may have some initial apprehension before he decides to enter it.This is when you will need a lot of patience.This is the stage wherein you want to ensure that your puppy will see the crate as a safe place and not as a cage.

So let's get down to the basics of how to get your puppy in and out of the crate without any hassles.

1. Bring the crate to the dog breeder's place and place it near you when you're spending time with your puppy.

2. Play with him for a bit and then lead him towards the crate. Never force the puppy into the crate. Use treats to engage his nose and allow his natural curiosity to follow your hand (with treats) into the crate. Allow him to get out again by enticing him with a treat.

Note: This process can take several attempts over the course of several visits. You have to be very patient at this point. The key here is to get your puppy accustomed to the presence of the crate. Getting in and out of the crate with ease is also part of the exercise to make your puppy feel safe with the crate around.

3. After your puppy is accustomed to the crate, it's time to practice closing the door on him while he is inside. Make sure that the puppy is in a relaxed state before you close the door of the crate. Never close the door on an agitated or over-excited

puppy as this could become a negative experience for him and may make him feel trapped inside the crate.

4. Allow the puppy to get out of the crate after several seconds. Repeat the process and make his stay inside the crate longer each time he successfully relaxes within the crate.

Note: once your puppy is extremely comfortable within the crate, you can now safely bring him home inside the crate.

As soon as you get home, simply lead the puppy out of the crate with treats. Give him lots of praise for coming out of the crate on his own.

Using the crate for potty training:

House breaking is an important part of your puppy's early life.

Crate training is an effective tool to housebreak your puppy. Just like any training session, extreme patience and vigilance is needed from here on out.

More details about housebreaking your puppy using crate training as the foundation   will be discussed under Chapter 3 – Housebreaking your puppy.

Using the crate to acclimate your puppy to its new surroundings

Removing your puppy from his familiar surroundings away from his mother and littermates is going to stress him out. So, now you have to deal with the responsibility of introducing each and every inch of your home to him bit by bit. Otherwise, your puppy is going to think he is free to go wherever and do whatever he wants in your own home. Puppies that are usually allowed to do this eventually grow up to become destructive dogs.This is not something that you would want to happen.

So let's use the crate to acclimatize your puppy to his new surroundings

1. First, place the crate in the smallest room you have and leave your puppy alone for a couple of minutes. You can also stay nearby where he can see or smell you so he doesn't feel too anxious about being left alone.

2. After a couple of minutes, when your puppy is totally relaxed, allow him to come out by his own or by using treats.

3. Allow your puppy to explore the room a bit. He'll be curious about all the new things and he'll be sniffing around. You have to be vigilant and make sure you look for any telltale signs that he may want to poop or urinate.

4. You can introduce your puppy to an adjoining room once he gets used to thatsmall room. Allow him to go from one room to another and only place him back in his crate if he gets anxious.

5. As your puppy grows older, introduce more rooms, but always keep the crate readily available so he always has a safe place to go back to when he gets anxious.

Using the crate to stop your puppy from being homesick

Homesickness is a common issue with puppies who are estranged from their mother and littermates. You'll know if he misses his family if he starts whimpering or howling when he is left alone. Don't worry, this is normal and crate training can be used to address this issue.

1. Place the crate beside your bed. Make sure you can easily reach it without having to get out of bed.

2. Tap the top of the crate lightly when your puppy starts whimpering or making a sound. This should snap him out of his current state of mind. This should immediately stop your puppy from making any noise.

3. Make sure you tap the crate immediately so that the puppy understands that you do not approve of the noise he is making. This will also assure him that you are nearby.

4. Over time, your puppy will become accustomed to his crate.His homesickness is going to stop and you'll have a peaceful night. Make sure you give your puppy a reward for being quiet all throughout the night.

Note: you can also use a spray can that shoots a light jet of water to hasten this process. Simply spray your puppy when he starts whimpering at night. A light spray should help quiet him down.

Another thing you can do to reduce your puppy's homesickness is to ask the dog breeder to give you a piece of cloth that has his mothers and siblings' scent on it. This should help ease the homesickness your puppy will experience during the first few days he is with you. Place a piece of cloth that has your scent in the crate as well so your puppy will get accustomed to you quickly.

Using the crate to stop your puppy from developing separation anxiety

Young puppies are extremely prone to developing separation anxiety. This can result in whimpering, barking or howling whenever you're away. This won't go over well if you live with neighbors next door who aren't too fond of too much racket coming from your place.

Since it is your responsibility to keep your dog quiet, you'll have to train him not to get too anxious when you're not around. Crate training is a great way to eliminate separation anxiety.

1. Place your puppy inside the crate and simply go about doing your regular basis. By this time your puppy should be comfortable being inside his crate training.

2. Move around but make sure that your puppy can see you at all times.Placing a toy inside the crate should help keep your puppy busy while you attend to your daily tasks.

3. Now, try to step out of sight for a minute or two and then come back to where your puppy can see you. Lengthen the time that you disappear as this training exercise progresses. Make sure to come back before your puppy becomes anxious over your absence.

As a general guideline, here are time approximations of the duration you can be absent before the puppy becomes anxious.

For puppies 9 to 10 weeks old, leave him alone for 30 minutes up to an hour. Make sure that the puppy is already accustomed to being inside the crate for at least 30 minutes before you start the exercise.

At 11 to 14 weeks old, you can leave your puppy from an hour to around 3 hours. At 15 to 16 weeks old, leaving him for a maximum of 4 hours won't bother him too much. This is the same for older dogs. Never leave your dog too long inside his crate.

Note: Never leave your dog inside the crate until he has calmed down during these training exercises.

Using crate training as a socializing tool for puppies

Dogs are among the most social creatures in the animal world. They thrive well in many situations where there are many interactions with people and other pets. But this does not come naturally especially for puppies. Socialization can be intimidating to puppies from the start. It is your responsibility to socialize your puppy properly and get him accustomed to the presence of other people and other pets without getting intimidated.

An improperly socialized animal can be a hassle in the future. You don't want your puppy to grow up into a fearful adult dog who will feel threatened around people or other animals.

You can use crate training to properly socialize your puppy so that you'll have a well-balanced dog in the future.

Socializing puppies to other people and family members

1. By now your puppy should be very comfortable staying inside his crate for extended periods of time venturing out only to empty his bowels, eat or exercise. There should be no signs of anxiety. This is the right time to introduce your puppy to people and other pets.

2. Place the crate in an area that receives some traffic from people and pets. Your puppy should be exposed to external stimuli without getting overloaded with the sights and sounds through this method.

3. Get a family member in your household to accompany you in the same room where the crate and the puppy are located. This will help your puppy identify the unique sound and smell this person possesses. This will also help your puppy realize that the person with you is not a threat and that there is nothing to be afraid of.

4. Entice the puppy to get out of the crate and approach the other person so he can get used to the smell and presence of another human being aside from you. Supervise the interaction between your puppy and that other person. At this point

touching the puppy is not necessary. After a couple of minutes allow the puppy to climb back into his crate. Reward your puppy with treats.

5. Continue adding more people to interact with your puppy. Always make sure that you reward your puppy with praise and treats. Let the other people in your household give treats as well.

Socializing puppies to other household pets

Socializing your puppy with other animals in your household can be tricky. But if this is done right, you'll have a more harmonious household.

1. Expose your puppy while he's in his crate to other animals in your household by placing his crate in an area frequented by other household pets.

2. Do not force any interaction just yet.

3. Allow the other pets to sniff around the crate.

4. Reward both your pet and your puppy for good behavior.

5. Continue this type of interaction several times before letting your puppy out to have some physical contact with your other pet. Make sure you supervise the interaction at all times to ensure no one gets hurt.

6. After a couple of minutes, separate the puppy from the other pet and place him back inside the crate.

7. Reward pets for good behavior if everything went smoothly.

Using crate training to make your puppy comfortable about traveling

Travelling is perhaps one of the most stressful events in any animal's life. Animals are used to travelling using their own feet. Travelling inside a vehicle can seem quite disconcerting and suffocating for any animal at first and it may take time for your pet to get accustomed to it.

You can use crate training to reduce the chances of your puppy getting stressed out during car trips or other forms of travel. Do this as early as possible so you won't have any issues when your puppy grows up.

1. Place the crate inside your vehicle and entice your puppy to climb into it using treats to engage his nose. Allow your puppy to climb in on his own. If he is too small, you might want to scoop him up and place him inside the car or provide a ramp. Make sure that he enters the crate on his own. This will take a lot of patience on your part.

2. Gently close the door to the crate once he is safely inside. Give your puppy some praises and rewards to get him into a calm and relaxed submissive state. Once your new puppy is relaxed

enough, you can now close the door to your car and start the engine.

3. Make sure you stop regularly to allow him to relieve himself or to stretch out every 30 minutes.

4. Once you've reached your intended destination, allow your puppy to come out of the crate by himself by engaging his nose with a treat. Make sure you reward your puppy with praise or treats to make travelling a very positive experience for him!All of these things may seem like a hassle for now but once your puppy gets used to travelling you'll see that it was all worth the effort!

In conclusion, crate training is a very important aspect in your puppy's development. It can address many issues in the future by instilling discipline at a very early age. Make sure you crate train your puppy to get a well-balanced dog in the future.

Remember to clean his crate regularly and to keep him inside for a maximum of 4 hours only.

Now let's move on to housebreaking your puppy and teaching him some basic commands in the next couple of chapters.

Chapter 3: Housebreaking your puppy

What is housebreaking and why is it so important?

Your puppy will eat voraciously for the first few months of his life and all that food has to come out of him somehow. This is why housebreaking is important. You do not want your house to become your puppy's personal toilet.

If you've already done the crate training for your puppy, this should be quite easy to do. Your puppy is not going to want to soil his immediate surroundings.

A Guide to housebreaking your puppy

To effectively housebreak your puppy, you will need to create a schedule that he can adhere to and look forward to every day.

Your puppy at 3 to 9 months old will need to eat at least 3 times a day (not including giving him treats and other goodies during training). You should potty train him right after every meal.

For now, you should control when he gets food and water to ensure that there won't be accidents happening inside your house. You will have to closely scrutinize his meal schedule as well.

This is an easy exercise that your puppy will easily learn within a couple of days.

First, take your puppy out of his crate and then give him his food during the scheduled time for his meal. It should also be a time when you're not in a rush as your puppy will need enough time to finish his food and do his business outside.

As soon as your puppy is done eating his meal, provide him with a bowl of clean water and allow him to drink his fill. When he is done, immediately lead your puppy outside either by using a leash or by telling him to follow you.

Lead him directly to his designated spot for eliminating waste and then wait for him to finish. Give your puppy a treat and a reward for a job well done when he's finished. Lead your puppy back into the house. Some puppies may not follow immediately and you may have to scoop him up to take him to his designated potty area. This is fine for now.

If you live in an apartment complex and you can't always readily bring your puppy outside after a meal, use old newspapers and place it in a corner. After he is done with his meal, place him in that area and wait for him to eliminate waste. When he is done give him a reward and praise him for a job well done. Discard the soiled newspapers but keep one piece that isn't entirely soaked through. Place a few sheets of fresh paper on top of it for the next time he needs to eliminate waste.

Always make it a point to reward your puppy and make him feel that he is doing a good job each time he does this so that he will know this is a behavior you like. Given enough time, your puppy will head to his designated potty area and do his business there without any prodding.

This should save you from picking up after your puppy each time he feels the call of nature coming to him after a meal.

You can also train your puppy to eliminate on demand. This is an advanced trick used by military and police personnel to ensure their dogs don't eliminate waste in public areas unplanned.

Assign a word that you don't normally use around the house to help "activate" your puppy's instinct to eliminate waste. For example: "Eliminate". Now, you have to be extra vigilant when your puppy is about to eliminate waste. When he is already in the process of defecating, repeat the word "eliminate" several times until he is done and then praise him and give him a treat. Repeat this process each time he does his business in his designated area. Over time, your puppy will associate the word "eliminate" for the right time to defecate and will only do his business if you give him the command.

The downside to this is that your puppy is going to wait for you each and every time to say the command before he does his business. This can pose a problem if you are not present at all times and your puppy needs to go out and make potty. So, only do this if you're sure you want a puppy that defecates only on command.

The same training can be applied for urinating. Simply repeat the process above but this time exchange the command for defecation with a command specifically for urinating.

Here is a more detailed explanation of the benefits of crate training for housebreaking your puppy:

Housebreaking your puppy using crate training:

1. Your puppy should now be comfortable within the confines of his crate. This is also the right time to start potty training. 15 to 20 minutes after your puppy has had a meal, take it outside and allow it to relieve itself. Remember to make this experience a very positive one with lots of treats and praise as a reward.

2. Return your puppy inside the crate and take him out every 20 minutes or so to relieve himself. Puppies have smaller bladders and although they don't want to poop or urinate inside their crate, they might not be able to hold it in for a long time.

3. If the puppy relieves himself when you go out, give him lots of praise and treats. If not, just return him to the crate and try again after a couple of minutes. This will take several attemptsand you have to be patient in order to get good results.

4. Make a definite schedule for your puppy to go outside to relieve himself so.

Be patient with your puppy if he unexpectedly poops or urinates inside hiscrate. Clean up the waste and then continue with crate training until you get the desired results.

Wash the entire crate thoroughly with lots of water. Use a non-ammonia cleaning liquid to remove the smell and reduce the risk of them doing it again in the same spot. Rinse thoroughly to remove any residue.

Chapter 4: Basic Obedience Training

There are 5 basic commands that your dog has to learn in order to become a well behaved dog. These commands are the "come", "sit", "down", "heel" and "stay" commands.

These are the universal commands that people are familiar with.

The "Come" command

The first command that your puppy should become well acquainted with is the come command. The "come" command can be used to familiarize your puppy with his name as well.

The "Sit" command

The second most important command to teach your puppy is the "sit" command.

The "Down" command

The down command is a bit harder to teach. Some dogs don't really like this command but given enough time and patience, this command is going to be very useful in disciplining your dog.

The "Heel" command

The heel command is a very important command that your puppy needs to learn. Sure it's easy to walk him right now that he's still small but if you wait long enough, he's going to grow into an adult and if he hasn't learned how to heel yet, you might have a potential walking issue on your hands.

You will need a lot of treats for this.

The "Stay" command

We've reserved this command last because it is the hardest to accomplish for both the trainer and the puppy. This command will require a lot of patience and positive reinforcement.

If you succeed in teaching your puppy how to stay on command, you'll have a very disciplined dog in the future. Furthermore, this training could take several days or weeks to accomplish so don't become frustrated and don't quit.

How to teach your puppy the "Come" command

The "come" command is very easy to teach. You will need a lot of treats and patience for this. You also have to ensure that you go into this training exercise with a high level of energy.

An added benefit to teaching the "come" command to your puppy is that he will also learn his name.

1. Open the crate door and entice your puppy out with a treat.

2. As soon as he is out of the crate, say "come". Allow your puppy to take the treat.

3. Take out another treat and entice him again to approach. Say the word "come" again. Give him the treat when he comes near.

4. Move a few steps away and hold out a treat and say "come". Give your puppy the treat when he successfully approaches you. Repeat the process, each time making the "come" command clear and giving him the treat when he comes near.

Add a few words of praise as a reward and patting to complement the food treat you are giving.

If you're using a clicker: click once as soon as you give him the treat. This should help him understand that he did a great job.

If you're using a whistle: gently blow on the whistle and say the command "come". Alternately use the whistle and using the "come" command. A whistle is a good tool to tell your dog to come when he is too far from you. This will also help you refrain from shouting at your dog to come back to you if he ever strays far from the path.

You can also use a hand gesture at this point. Raise your hand in front of you with your palm facing inwards. Fold your arm in while retaining a vertical position to complement the command.

To teach your puppy how to recognize his name with the "come" command; add his name after saying come. Note: only do this when he has fully recognized the command "come".

So when you say "come" add his name to the command. So it should be "come, fido" or "come, spot".

Make sure that he understands the difference between the come command with his name and simply saying his name. You don't want your puppy to approach every time he hears his name.

As this training exercise progresses, you can have other people emulate what you are doing so that your puppy will go to them when they say "come". A great exercise is having another person stand at another end of the room and you can alternately call the puppy to come to whoever is issuing the command.

How to teach your puppy the "Sit" command

The second most important command to teach your puppy is the "sit" command. This can easily be done using the blocking technique and a raised platform.

1. Have your puppy directly in front of you. You can use a raised platform to make this easier.

2. Have a treat in your hand and place it in front of your puppy's nose. As soon as it gets his attention, raise your hand. He will naturally follow the scent which should make him look up. Your hand should be at least 3 inches above his head for now.

3. This motion will make his body instinctively follow his head which should put him in a sitting position. As soon as his rump touches the floor (or table surface) say "Sit" and then hand him the treat.

4. Allow your puppy to stand again and repeat the process until he makes the connection between his rump touching the floor and the command "sit".

5. The next part of this training exercise is to place him on the floor directly in front of you and repeat the command but this time raising your hand even higher.

Use a hand gesture with the sit command. The proper hand gesture for this is an outwardly facing hand with your index finger pointed up. Keep your other fingers closed to hold on to the treat inside your palm.

To use the blocking technique, you can simply step forward until you are directly in front of your puppy. Use the hand gesture to complement this blocking technique.

Try to do this exercise in a place where there are no distractions.

For puppies who find it hard to understand the "sit" command you can tap their rump to bring attention to that body part. Lightly push down to encourage a sitting position and then say the command"sit". Use this method sparingly as your puppy might associate this touching motion as a reward. It should only be used to get an initial reaction.

Remember to reward your puppy as soon as he sits on command.

How to teach your puppy the "Down" command

The "down" command is basically a modified "sit" command. What this basically does is tell your dog to lie flat on the floor (without rolling over). This is an extremely good command as it will also encourage your dog to relax if he is feeling hyperactive.

You can practice this command if your puppy has already learned how to sit or if your dog has a natural propensity to lie down when he comes near you.

If he is a submissive dog, he will immediately lie down in front of you. Encourage this behaviour by giving him a reward and giving the "down" command at the same time.

Here's how you can teach your dog to follow the "down" command:

1. Call your puppy to come to you. Once he is in front of you issue the command "down". Use a hand gesture with your arm out and your palm facing the ground. At the same time that you issue the command "down" make a downward motion with your hand.

2. If your puppy already knows how to sit, he might follow your command with a sitting motion. Do not give him a treat at this point. Wait for your puppy to feel a bit curious as to why he has not received his treat yet. There'll be some tail wagging as he anticipates a treat at this point. Repeat the command. His natural tendency at this point is to become submissive and beg for the treat. His natural instinct will be to get even lower than his normal sitting position. The next thing that should happen is your puppy lying down with his head still intently looking at your hand waiting for the treat.

3. As soon as he lies down, say the command "down" again and give him a treat. Repeat the process.

4. This training exercise has a progression. Each time he lies down he will still be excited to get his treat. To remove this excess excitement, withhold the treat after he has learned what the command "down" means. Wait for your puppy to relax a bit before giving him a treat. Make this sessions longer to effectively wait for your puppy to relax. By the end of this exercise, your puppy should know that he has to lie down and relax in order to get a treat.

Lying down is not an easy command for dogs to learn;many dogs find it difficult to learn. You will have to be very patient with your puppy so that he will learn this command and lie down when you ask him to.

How to teach your puppy the "Heel" command

The "heel" command is an easy command to teach your puppy especially if you take him out regularly to exercise.

This will require a lot of treats and patience on your end. You can also start this exercise with a leash to keep your puppy from straying too far.

To walk your dog properly, make sure he knows staying beside you is better than straying too far from you. You might want to give your dog a short jog before starting this exercise to wean off the excess energy he has or to tire him out a bit.

1. When you take your puppy out for a walk, make sure that you practice proper blocking to make sure he does not pull at the leash. If he tries to get ahead use your leg or a walking cane to block him so that he stays abreast of you and not ahead of you. If he pulls towards the side, stop and command him to come to you.

2. Starting from a sitting position, give the command to "heel" and start walking. Your puppy should stay directly beside you. Keep him at the side where your hand is holding onto the leash. Make sure you have a treat in this hand to attract him to stay at that side. Give him a treat every two steps you take. When you give him a treat, repeat the command "heel". Use a hand gesture at this time to signify where you want him to stay. A closed hand with an extended index finger is the hand gesture to use during this exercise.

3. Continue walking normally giving the command "heel" at the same time while providing him the treats. This should form an association in his brain that as long as he stays on the side where your leash hand is (the hand with the extended index finger) he will get a treat.

4. When he becomes accustomed to the command, try issuing the "heel" command while he is off-leash. Only provide treats when he successfully follows the command. Try doing this in a controlled environment first before moving on to the outdoors where there are a lot of distractions.

You can use this command to make your puppy less apprehensive of sounds outside your home. Try doing this exercise while traversing a busy sidewalk. Be vigilant at this point and make sure he heels whenever he feels too curious. Stop walking if he does not listen to you.

You can also use a whistle at this point to call him back to you if he strays too far. As soon as he is near you give the command to "heel" so he understands that this means he has to stay by your side at all times.

How to teach your puppy the "Stay" command

The "stay" command is perhaps the hardest command to teach your puppy. With enough patience you can successfully teach your puppy to stay on command.

Before teaching this command, you should make sure that your puppy already knows how to "sit" on command.

1. Command your puppy to "sit" directly in front of you.

2. Now step back and command your puppy to "stay". Use a hand gesture for this. Stretch out your arm in front of you with your palm facing your puppy directly so he will understand the command through this physical gesture. Wait a couple of seconds before stepping forward and giving your puppy a treat.

3. Repeat the process but this time take two steps back and wait a couple seconds more before stepping forward again to reward your puppy.

4. Make sure that your puppy remains relaxed at this time without any signs of anxiety as he waits for his treat. If he shows any unnecessary excitement, step forward and wait for him to calm down before issuing the command again.

5. As this training exercise progresses, move further away from your puppy while issuing the command and wait longer times before giving him a reward.

Make sure that this training exercise is done in a room where there are no distractions present so your puppy can concentrate. When he begins to understand this command, you can transfer him to a room that has other people in it.

Once he fully understands the command, allow other people to give the command.

You can also use the blocking technique to train your puppy to stay during this training exercise. What you need to do is block him first and then issue the command to stay. After that, move away and repeat the command. If he stays in the same position give him a reward. If he tries to follow you, step forward and block him.

Teaching your puppy how to obey these 5 basic commands will produce a well behaved puppy who will eventually grow up to be a well-balanced dog in the future.

Advanced commands for your puppy

These commands will make your life easier with your dog. Although they serve a purpose (example: taking a bath easily) they are not categorized as a basic command.

Training your puppy to love taking a bath

Puppies are not really that fond of getting wet. If you do not train your puppy early on in life to love taking a bath, you might have an issue with keeping him clean once he becomes a full grown dog.

You do not want to be wrestling with a 15lb dog just to keep him clean.

You need to start him off in the right direction. Have the dog shampoo and wash cloth ready with a lot of treats to get him used to this activity.

1. The most important thing to do is to form an association in his mind that bath time is a pleasurable activity. So, present the dog shampoo to him while you're spending time with him. Allow him to sniff the shampoo. As soon as he does that give him a treat and say the command "bath".
2. Allow him to get comfortable with the scent of dog shampoo. Make sure he associates it as part of a pleasurable activity by giving him lots of treats each time he sniffs it.
3. Next, have some running water nearby. Get him accustomed to the sound of running water so that he does not panic when he hears it. Give him a treat to make an association in his mind that this is part of a pleasurable activity. Keep saying the command "bath" all throughout this activity.

4. Now, take a wash cloth and wet it with some water. Wipe your dog lightly while saying "bath" and giving him a treat for good behavior.

5. This may take several tries before he relaxes when there is water so patience is the key to getting him accustomed to taking a bath.

6. As soon as your puppy is comfortable with the running water and the scent of the dog shampoo, it is time to give him a proper bath. Simply lift your puppy and place him in the tub or basin with some water in it. It should be deep enough to reach his belly. You might want to have someone assisting you with this activity so that treats can continually be given while you give the command "bath".

7. Clean your puppy using slow motions to pour water all over his back and using light but firm strokes to lather him up with the shampoo.

8. Rinse of your puppy completely and give him a reward for the good behavior after the bath.

You can also include the use of a shower head to get your puppy used to being cleaned with soft jets of water. This is going to be very useful when your puppy is fully grown up and all he needs is a simple hosing down to clean him up.

For frisky puppies, keep calm and be patient. If he moves around a lot, stop giving him a treat and stop moving. Keep him still by holding on to him firmly. As soon as he relaxes continue the cleaning motion and giving rewards.

Use non-toxic shampoo to clean your pet and always make sure that the water is warm enough for his comfort.

Give your puppy a bath sparingly. A bath once or twice a month should be enough for your puppy. When he is older, giving him a bath once a month should be enough.

Training your puppy to love getting groomed

Logically, the next thing you need to teach your puppy is how to love being groomed on a regular basis. After his bath, this is the best time to groom your dog. Grooming your dog should include cleaning his fur, clipping his claws and checking his dental health.

You will need a lot of treats at this point to get him to love this activity. You will also need to get him accustomed to the items used for grooming before you actually groom him. You can do this at the same time that you present the bath items.

If you intend to use a hair dryer, try to turn it on a few feet away from him so that he does not get startled by the sound. As soon as the hair dryer is turned on, assure your puppy and give him a treat to calm him down. As this training exercise progresses, get him nearer to the hair dryer all the while giving him a treat to reward him for not panicking. Soon enough you should have a puppy who is comfortable being around the noisy hair dryer without being afraid of the contraption.

1. As soon as he is done with his bath, wipe him dry with a bath towel.
2. This is the right time to clean his ears with some cotton buds or by simply wrapping your finger with a paper towel and swabbing around his ear. Take care not to push too hard as it may damage the internal organs inside his ears.

3. Next, use the blow dryer to completely dry your puppy. He should be used by now to the sound of the hair dryer. Make sure you put an emphasis of giving him rewards for good behavior at this stage.

4. Run a wide toothed comb through his fur to remove any tangles. For extremely matted fur, get a pair of scissors and cut the problem area. Trying to disentangle this snarled fur is going to be painful for your puppy and this may cause a negative association if he feels any pain during the grooming session at this point of his life.

5. Next, run a fine toothed comb to further smooth out his fur. This is also the best time to check for any mites, ticks and other parasites on his skin.

6. Apply a light dusting of flea powder to remove any parasites present.

7. Next, check his claws and clip them if they have become too long. Make sure that you take great care not to hit the quick as this can cause great pain to your puppy. File the claws to achieve a blunt edge and apply a thin lacquer film to protect it from any damage. You can also encourage your puppy to dig through hard soil to keep his claws blunt.

8. Check his eyes for any redness and his eye lids. His eyelids should have a dark pink hue. This signifies good health. If his lower eyelids are pale, take him to a vet.

9. Check his nose, make sure there is no mucus build up and that it is slightly damp. Apply petroleum jelly to your puppy's nose to protect it from sun damage.

10. Pry your puppy's mouth open and check his oral health. Next, check his teeth for any tartar build up or cavities. You can clean your puppy's mouth with a finger brush and a good amount of canine dental care solution.

Give your puppy a reward for being patient all throughout the grooming session. In fact, your puppy should constantly be supplied with treats as the grooming session is going on. This will help him associate this process as a pleasurable activity. As he grows older you'll find out that he won't need as many treats and a few positive encouragements and rubbing on his head is enough to satisfy his need for a reward.

Training your puppy to love going to the vet and taking his medicines

One of the toughest aspects of taking care of any pet is taking care of his health. Puppies are especially prone to getting sick because of their curious nature and adventurous spirit.

It is a known fact that pets also seem to hate going to the vet or taking their medicines.

You can easily turn this situation around by making trips to the vet a pleasurable one. One way to do this is to not make a big fuss about the visit to the vet. Make it seem like a normal routine you go through with your pet.

Make it a point to make a social visit to your pet and don't just go there because something's wrong with your puppy.

1. Call your vet ahead of time and schedule a social visit. Inform your vet that you want to properly introduce the puppy to him for socialization purposes.
2. Once you are at or near the veterinarian's clinic, take your puppy for a quick walk around the block to wean off his excess energy.

3. As soon as you're done with the brief exercise, enter the veterinarian's clinic (during the appointed time for your social visit). Make sure you take on a very positive energy so that your puppy will associate entering the vet's clinic as part of a good experience or adventure.

4. Allow your vet to pet your puppy, give him a treat and basically do a quick look over. Allow your vet to place your puppy up on the examination table for a brief moment of time so that he can get used to the feeling of being there. If you've properly done the training for the "sit" command, this should be an easy thing to do as your puppy already associates being off the ground as a way to get treats. Make sure your vet gives him a treat for behaving properly on top of the examination table.

5. After a few minutes, take your puppy down and give him another treat for behaving properly.

If you do this several times a week, your puppy should be able to associate visits to the vet as a pleasurable event instead of a stressful one. The key here is to properly socialize your pet with your vet so that he won't feel any fear when he has to go to the clinic.

Giving your dog his medicine can be a stressful event if you don't train him to take his vitamins without forcing him. You can address this concern by simply making it a fun activity for him. One way to do this is to sandwich his vitamins in between treats.

Get your dog's energy up by playing with him. Once his energy is sufficiently up, try doing the "sit" command with him. Now, instead of handing him the treat by hand, toss it up in the air and let him catch it with his mouth.

Give him the command to "sit" several times. Each time he acts properly, give him a treat. In between the command, walk away and ask him to come to you and then tell him to "sit" again.

This is a fun exercise for your pet and he will have his attention trained on you the whole time. Now, in between treats (let's say every three treats) toss him one of his vitamins for him to catch with his mouth. Make sure that when you toss the medicine in the air you utter the command "meds". At first, he won't notice the difference between the treats and the medicines because of his excitement level. He'll easily gobble it down without any fuss. After he takes his medicine, give him another treat for the good behavior.

If your dog gets accustomed to taking his medicines in this manner, you won't have any issue getting him to swallow the pill. Make it a fun activity and you'll never have to worry about forcing medicines down his throat just so you can keep him healthy.

For liquids, mix the medicine in the water he drinks and keep a watchful eye as he drinks the entire concoction down. You might want to encourage him by praising him as he drinks the medicine down. After he is done, give him another treat for good behavior.

There are some puppies that are especially hard to administer vitamins to. Some owners resort to dirty tactics like inserting the medicine inside a piece of meat. This is also a good practice that you might want to look into adding to your own bag of tricks to keep your dog healthy.

Teaching your puppy how to "fetch" and "give"

One trick that dog owners would love to have their puppies learn is how to fetch. Now you have to understand that not all dogs have the predisposition to do so. Some may chase after the ball and not give it back and there are some dogs that won't even bother to chase the ball at all!

Play to your dog's strengths. Do not expect a toy dog to go bounding after a ball to give it back to you. This trick works best with working or hunting dog breeds. Still, it's worth giving it a shot.

1. Find a toy that your puppy is especially attached to and hold it in front of him to get his attention. Once he has his sights trained on the toy, throw it a few feet away from and give the command to "fetch".
2. Don't worry if your dog is surprised with this action. His natural instinct will tell him to go after the toy.
3. Once he reaches his toy, tell your dog to "come". This is a hit or miss situation as he may come with the toy in his mouth or he may choose to leave it to obey your command. If he leaves the toy and comes to you, give him a treat for obeying the command to "come" and then tell him to "stay" while you pick the toy up. Repeat the process of getting his attention and throwing the toy away again for a short distance.
4. If he brings the toy with him when he obeys the command to "come", ask for the toy back by stretching your arm out with your palm facing upward. Now give the command to "give". If he drops the toy, give him a treat and praise him for the good behavior. If he decides to hang on to the toy, place a treat near his nose and repeat the command "give" until he drops the toy in favor of getting the treat.

5. Repeat the process making sure that you give the "fetch" command as clearly as you can and asking for the toy back by saying "give". For each successful attempt make sure to reward your dog profusely with treats and praises.

Teaching your dog how to fetch is a great way to exercise your dog which makes it a very important command to train your dog with. As this training exercise progresses, throw the toy further and further away. You can also assign a specific toy for fetching like a ball which should travel further away from your pet when thrown. The bouncing action as the ball lands will also help to excite your dog even further which should make this exercise an extremely fun activity for you and your puppy.

Teaching your pet how to "give" something back will also help to assert your dominance as well as curb any aggressiveness issue that you may have with your pup during his growing stages.

Chapter 5: Correcting Your Puppy's Bad Behavior

Your puppy has no concept of right or wrong when you first get him. It is part of your responsibility to correct bad behavior immediately so that this does not become a bad habit in the future.

There are many ways to correct bad behavior. You can use the spoken word method or using a tool like a spray to get his attention. As a last resort, you can use a physical method to immediately correct hard headed puppies. This is to be used only when you've exhausted all means to get his attention and redirect his energy.

Teaching your puppy the meaning of "no"

One very important command that your puppy should understand is the word "no". He should be able to understand that this means you do not approve of his action. You can also use a sharp "Tsssh" sound that Cesar Millan has popularized in his Dog Whisperer show.

You will have to be very vigilant at this point to ensure that any bad behavior is reprimanded immediately.

To do this, simply let your puppy go about his business but keep a watchful eye at all times. If you notice anything that you don't want him to do, immediately reprimand him by saying "no" or "tsssh" to get his attention. Your puppy should look towards you at this point. Redirect him so that he does not repeat the behavior.

Using a water spray to correct bad behavior

You can also use a water spray to correct his behavior. This does not harm your dog and serves only to snap him out of his current state of mind.

To do this, allow your puppy to go about his business and keep a watchful eye for anything he might do that you don't approve of. Once he starts misbehaving spray him once. You can also complement this action by using the spoken word "no" or "tsssh".

Done enough times, your puppy should be able to associate bad behaviours with getting wet. If you do this training exercise properly, your dog will have second thoughts of doing something bad in fear of getting wet.

Using physical actions to correct bad behavior

As a last resort, you may want to use physical measures to correct your dog. This can be done by giving him a sharp poke near the junction where his armpit and his chest meet. This can immediately snap him out of his current state of mind.

Using your index and middle finger, simulate a claw or dog's mouth and give him a sharp jab enough to snap him out of his current state of mind.

This is a method used by the dog whisperer and has shown great results.

Using an e-collar to correct bad behavior

This is a polarizing topic as there are people who are extremely against the idea of using an e-collar on their precious pets.

An e-collar is a collar that delivers an electric shock to the puppy when you click on the button to activate it. This is actually a modernized version of the more medieval training choke collar or pronged collars which is just as painful when used.

There are advantages and disadvantages to using an e-collar. For extremely hard to train or red line dogs, this can be an effective tool to get their attention to correct bad behavior.

Make sure that your puppy only receives a short jolt with just the right amount of voltage to correct bad behavior. This can be very traumatizing for your pet so only use this as the very last resort.

Using bitter sprays to correct bad behavior

This is an extremely messy method but it is just as effective as using a spray. This is good for correcting biting behaviors.

Puppies go through a teething stage and this can cause them to look for things to bite on to relieve the pain that comes along with growing their teeth. Unfortunately, puppies often bite on things they're not supposed to as opposed to biting on a proper teething tool. This can cause damage to furniture, shoes, toys and other precious items within his mouth's range inside your house.

To correct this, you might want to wipe bitter fluid or wax on furniture so that when he bites on it, he'll get a bitter taste in his mouth. This can be very annoying for your puppy and he will think twice the next time he wants to bite on something.

To encourage him to bite on a proper teething toy, wipe the toy with some tasty oil. Used cooking oil will retain some of the taste of the food it was used to cook. It will also retain the smell from the food. This can be extremely attractive to your puppy which should encourage him to bite on the teething toy instead of other items in your house.

You can also train him to bite on the teething toy by giving it to him and then giving him a reward for biting it. Simply present the toy to him. When he bites on it, give him a reward and then allow him to return to the toy to bite on it. Give him a reward from time to time to give him an association of pleasure with the toy.

Chapter 6: Additional Tips To Becoming A Good Trainer And Making Sure Your Puppy Follows Every Command You Give

Take your dog for a walk

There is nothing that a dog loves more than taking a walk. Taking a walk can give them the exercise they need to wean off their excess energy. Taking a walk also gives them some structure which should emphasize your role as the alpha in your relationship with him.

Take your dog out for a walk once or twice a day. A 30 minute walk should be enough to tire your dog out.

Walking your dog before any training sessions can also help motivate your dog to become receptive to the training methods mentioned in the previous chapters.

Play with your dog

After your training sessions, make it a point to play with your dog. Training can only go so far and your dog will need to play to keep him happy. Throwing a ball for him to chase or wrestling with your dog is a good way of playing with him.

Take note of your dog's excitement level and correct bad behaviors immediately. Reprimand your dog if he starts biting or nipping if he gets excited. You do not want to promote this type of behavior as it could pose a problem in the future.

Train your dog in a place free from distractions

You want your puppy's full attention on you at all times during the training session. So, make sure you do your trainings initially in an environment away from distractions.

Get to know your dog better

One way to become a better trainer is to get to know your puppy better. He is an individual and he has his own unique traits. Use these unique traits to your advantages.

Some puppies can be trained to do certain tricks faster if they have a natural inclination to perform the trick. For example: giving a paw can be reinforced if your puppy raises his paw to get your attention. To do this, simply give him the command "paw" whenever he raises his paw to reach out to you. Make sure you give him a reward to associate it as a good behavior.

Time your training sessions

Quality over quantity is the key to having a great training session. Keep your training sessions short so that you can maintain your puppy's motivation and attention. Studies have shown that keeping your training sessions under 15 minutes show better results than training sessions that take longer. Make sure that you focus each training session on a certain command until he fully understands it and then complement the training session with other commands that he is already familiar with.

For newer commands, try to keep the focus on learning the command during that time.

Be the leader of the pack

In the wild, wolves and dogs form packs as a form of security. Young puppies learn by emulating the actions of the older dogs in the pack. They are also corrected immediately if they do not follow instructions immediately.

This is basically the same thing within your home. To effectively train your puppy, be the leader of the pack.

Reward your dog's good behavior

To encourage good behavior, always make sure that you reward your dog. Be mindful of what he is doing and always keep a treat on you or nearby so you can immediately heap him with rewards for good behaviors.

Doing this several times should help him form an association in his mind that this type of behavior is rewarded and he will do it constantly to get the treats in your hand.

Timing is the key

Proper timing should be practiced at all times so you can catch your puppy if he is doing something good or bad. It goes without saying that proper behavior should be rewarded while negative behaviors should be reprimanded.

Never reinforce undesirable behavior

Some negative behaviors puppies do may seem cute and harmless during his early years. This should never be reinforced as it could become a big problem in the future.

Excessive play barking for instance is one type of behavior that may seem cute. Now imagine your puppy as a grown up dog with a louder bark. If he gets excited he is going to bark and it can be a nuisance for you and your neighbors if he barks incessantly during play time.

Training your dog is a day to day activity

Training your dog is not something that you do on a whim. This is part of your ongoing commitment to raising your puppy right.

This means you will have to train your pup on a daily basis. There are no exceptions, if you simply cannot do it because of a health issue, have someone else in your family spend time training your dog for you.

Training your dog daily makes it an activity for your dog to look forward to. This ensures that he is always motivated and will keep his mind from getting bored.

Use one syllable word commands at the beginning

Use one syllable word commands so that your dog easily understands what is expected of him. If you've noticed, the basic commands are one syllable words.

Treat it as an emulation of how your pup would interact with another dog in the pack. Dogs communicate using short barks or yelps to tell one another what to do.

Focus on one command at a time

Focus on one command at a time to make it easier for your puppy to understand what it is you want him to do. As soon as he learns the lesson by heart, mix it up to check for further understanding.

Recognize the fact that all dogs are different

One great thing about dogs is that they come in all shapes and sizes. They also come with specific personalities and quirks. But, there is a good way to gauge what your dog is capable of doing by learning more about the breed and the class he belongs to.

Here's a basic rundown of breeds and classes and other pertinent information:

The sporting group

This is a great breed for people who live an active lifestyle and want to own a puppy who can reflect the same amount of energy. The sporting group is easy to train as they are highly motivated to perform and they have the energy to match their eagerness.

Expect these dogs to do well with walking exercises related training and fetching stuff.

The hound group

These are the seekers in the dog world equipped with the most powerful noses. These dogs do well in situations where they have to find something and bring it back to you. Play to this breeds strengths by keeping them occupied with tricks and training exercises that engage their sense of smell.

These dogs are also very easy to entice with treats as their powerful noses can smell hidden treats in your palm or in containers hidden from view.

The working group

These dogs easily get bored if they don't have anything to do. These dogs thrive well in training situations as it gives them something to focus on. Their high energy and motivation levels will also help them last through longer training sessions than most dogs.

Working dogs are fun to work with because they are very eager to learn and please their master. They are also highly capable of learning complex tricks that other groups may not be able to learn easily.

A downside to having a working dog is their tendency to become destructive when they get bored. So make it a point to give them regular exercise and training sessions so you won't end up with a destroyed home.

The terrier group

This group is a fun bunch as they are always amped. These dogs have very high energy levels and are on par with that of a working dog's energy level.

Terriers are also very eager to please and thrive in training situations. In fact, terriers are often lumped in with working dogs because these little pups love to perform specific chores like hunting and chasing down balls and other moving toys.

Give them as much exercise as a working dog and you should have a very contented terrier snoring by your side at night. Don't expect them to sleep soundly though because any sound (no matter how faint it may seem) is bound to get them up and alert within seconds to investigate!

The toy group

The toy group is often thought of as lazy dogs but this is far from the truth as most of the dogs lumped into this category also belong to the terrier group.

The toy group can be very energetic but they do tire out easily because of how their bodies are built.

Still, that's no excuse to not give them some form of exercise.

Dogs belonging in the toy group are very territorial so you will have to make sure that you weed out their aggressive tendencies by socializing them properly. Do not fall for their charms as you might end up with a dog who is jealous of anyone else giving you attention.

Dogs belonging to the toy group are also incessant barkers so make sure you address this by using the spray method to keep them from barking without any reason for hours on end.

The non-sporting group

These dogs are perfect for people who have very low energy levels. These dogs love to lounge around and just stay chill.

Teach these dogs the basic commands but don't expect them to follow immediately.

These dogs would rather sleep than fetch a ball. So keep your training sessions short enough to keep their attention on you and leave them alone for the rest of the day.

Since these dogs have a tendency to get fat from the lack of activity, make it a point to put them on a strict diet and to give them some minimal exercise to keep them healthy.

The herding group

This is an offshoot of the working dog group. Treat these dogs like working dogs and you won't have any issues with destructive tendencies.

The mixed breed group

The view on mixed breeds has changed over the course of time and people are now more open to adopting mixed breeds instead of just purebred dogs. Mixed breed dogs appear to be stronger than their counterparts and have better overall health than purebreds.

It is also fun getting to know a mixed breed because you'll never know what you'll get. He may retain certain characteristics from one or two parents and his personality may also be a mixture of his predecessors.

Make it a point to research both breeds that your mixed breed belongs to so that you have a good idea of what to expect and then train him according to his natural strengths.

Learn more about your dog

If you want to get to know your dog better, take the time to learn more about him. There are many educational materials that can help point you in the right direction. You can visit your local library and check for books specifically targeted at the breed or you can scour the internet for every tidbit of information that can help you know more about your dog.

There are many types of dogs and each specific breed comes with his or her own specific quirks. You can use the information you learn to address his weaknesses and play to his strengths. This should in turn make training an easier process because you have a better understanding of what makes your dog tick.

Watch expert trainers do their work

Reading about training methods can only take you so far. You might want to enhance your innate talent in training dogs by learning from the experts.

Watch how expert dog trainers operate and take note of how they train their dog and emulate what they are doing.

Better yet you can contact an expert dog trainer and ask him to teach you how to train your dog properly. You may have to pay him for his services but learning how to properly train your dog is something that is priceless!

Don't flick your dog's nose

Have you ever had your nose hit? It stings right?

That's basically the same for your puppy. Except dogs noses are more sensitive to human beings. Dogs' noses are full of nerves and cavities which makes it an efficient tool in finding hidden stuff or recognizing one another.

Flicking your pup's nose is a very traumatic event and your puppy will remember the pain associated with it. This may build some distrust between you and your puppy which could impede your training progress.

So, never, ever flick your dog's nose.

Last but not the least: Love your dog and your dog will love you

This is the most important part of owning a dog. Give your puppy lots of love and you can be sure that he will give you back the same amount of love if not more! There is nothing that can compare to a dog's love for his human. It is an unconditional love that nothing short of death can stop.

Conclusion

I hope this book was able to help you to understand your puppy better and become a better trainer than when you first started.

The next step is to use the steps provided in this book to make your puppy a well rounded. Be patient, be consistent and make sure you give him lots of rewards and you should see a marked improvement in his general behavior!

I wish you the best of luck.

Alex Rutters

Made in the USA
Columbia, SC
11 March 2023

13631202R00043